RIVERSIDE COMMUNITY COLLEGE
1916
D0576746

FEDERALISM and CIVIL RIGHTS

FEDERALISM and CIVIL RIGHTS

BY BURKE MARSHALL

FOREWORD BY ROBERT F. KENNEDY

COLUMBIA UNIVERSITY PRESS

NEW YORK AND LONDON

1964

Burke Marshall is Assistant Attorney General,
Civil Rights Division, Department of Justice.

LIBRARY OF CONGRESS CATALOG CARD NUMBER: 64-7533
MANUFACTURED IN THE UNITED STATES OF AMERICA

TO MY WIFE

THE GINO SPERANZA LECTURES

This book is based on the Gino Speranza Lectures for 1964, delivered at Columbia University in March and April, 1964.

The Gino Speranza Lecture Fund was established in 1952 by a bequest of Mr. Speranza's wife, the late Florence Colgate Speranza, to provide annual lectures devoted to "American traditions and ideals, viewed from an historical viewpoint."

Foreword

One of the most difficult problems the Department of Justice has had to face during the past three and a half years is how to explain the apparent anomaly of having sent marshals and soldiers to Oxford, Mississippi, in September 1962 and not having done so during the civil rights crisis in Birmingham, Alabama, in May 1963; of having sent marshals to Montgomery, Alabama, in May 1961 when the Freedom Riders were beaten but not to Mississippi in the summer of 1964 as violence over racial matters increased and three young civil rights workers disappeared.

The marshals and soldiers were sent to Oxford to prevent interference with federal court orders that James Meredith should be admitted to the University of Mississippi. The marshals went to the aid of the Freedom Riders because Alabama authorities either could not or would not protect persons traveling in interstate commerce. In both situations, there was clear federal responsibility. This was not the case at Birmingham in May 1963 or as of July 15, 1964, in the movement of young civil rights workers into Mississippi.

In this book Mr. Marshall discusses the anomaly and the practical questions—arising out of our basic federal constitutional system—that the civil rights struggle of the 1960s has created. Our forefathers devised a system of checks and balances. They were concerned lest too much power be placed in the hands of one group within the federal government. Therefore, they divided the government into three separate branches: the executive, the legislative, and the judiciary. As a check on all three branches as a whole, they left considerable power to the states as separate entities. One of these powers was responsibility for maintaining law and order.

The United States is one of the few countries in the world that does not have a national police force. The federal government was not given any general police power unless a state's ability to maintain law and order had broken down. This was another protection for individual citizens and for the states themselves, and up to this time the concept has always been accepted and has had strong support in every part of the nation.

But the intricacies of our federal system and the distinctions between when and how the federal government can act are difficult to explain to a nation sickened and aroused by photographs and news accounts of a police dog at the throat of a Negro woman and of a fire hose knocking over a Negro child. Careful explanations of the historic limitations on the federal government's police powers are not satisfactory to the parents of students who have vanished in Mississippi or to the widow of a Negro educator shot down without any reason by night riders in Georgia.

Accordingly, there is an increasing demand on the part of our people for federal protection of our Negro citizens in some areas in the South, as well as protection for those working with them on behalf of civil rights. At the same time, there is a reluctance to start down the path that would lead inevitably to the creation of a national police force.

In this book Mr. Marshall has described the heartless, organized mistreatment of our fellow Americans who are Negroes that has caused such great consternation in the country. A Negro arrested for parading without a permit because, walking by himself, he has "freedom now" written on his shirt; Negroes by the tens of thousands denied the right to register and vote in elections in an area extending across northern Louisiana and through most of Mississippi and a large section of Alabama; or a Negro beaten with the butt of a gun and then arrested for disorderly conduct when he attempted to register to vote: these incidents strike at our national conscience.

Should the role of the federal government be merely to stand by and let these activities continue? The decision to use marshals or troops against the wishes of a state government and a substantial proportion of the citizens of the state is one of the most difficult decisions that an attorney general must recommend and that a president must make. This is a dilemma not only for the president to resolve and for the Department of Justice to deal with, but for all our people to ponder.

Burke Marshall was one of the late President Kennedy's most valued advisers. He was closely involved with President Kennedy in all of the decisions dealing with civil rights, and he has continued in this role under President Johnson. Mr. Marshall has discussed the subject of federal versus state responsibility in a brilliant and articulate way, based on his considerable experience over the past three and a half years and fortified by years of study.

Mr. Marshall has rendered invaluable service to the American people. And now, with the publication of this book, written with insight and giving perspective to one of the most difficult problems facing our country, he has made another important contribution.

ROBERT F. KENNEDY
Attorney General of the United States

July 15, 1964

Contents

FEDERALISM and CIVIL RIGHTS

☆

Introduction

In the 1963 lectures of this series Theodore Sorensen analyzed the factors which shape the decisions of the President. His emphasis was on dilution of presidential powers, not on their reach. When the lectures were published, President Kennedy wrote in a foreword of the "extraordinary limitations" which bound the "extraordinary powers" of the Presidency, and "which so often give the problem of choice its complexity and even poignancy." Mr. Sorensen also began by identifying not the sources of power, but the "outer limits of decision"—the limits of permissibility, available resources, available time, previous commitments, and available information.

President Kennedy decided during his term of office that racial discrimination had to be eliminated as an official or accepted course of society in every part of the United States. This was a profoundly significant decision, of expanding dimensions, defying to some degree all of the outer limits of decisions, the meaning of which cannot yet be discussed without presumption and understatement. The consequences of an intensive effort against official racial discrimination in the South alone are too diverse and complicated to be clearly discerned now. The President went further to seek a national commitment to meet the moral dilemma caused by the effects of our historical acceptance of a caste system weighted against Negroes. In doing so he set into motion a new test of the ability of the federal system finally to face problems that had been a primary cause of the dissolution of the Union, that had proved insoluble by Reconstruction, and that have been partially or completely obscured since.

It is apparent that this undertaking is not one that can be accomplished by the federal government. The President did request comprehensive legislation, now under consideration by Congress, treating those aspects of racial discrimination that can be reached by federal law. In a series of White House meetings, he also asked the help of all segments of national leadership, public and private, in facing such deep economic, social, and educational racial problems as those of the great cities where federal, state, and municipal policy in general coalesce, rather than clash, but no solution is yet in sight. Many thousands, probably hundreds of thousands, of citizens became involved in the effort as a result.

The nation is presently engaged in resolving the issue, using the full diversity and disunity of the forces that determine our history to do so. In the meantime, the polarization of Negro and other civil rights leadership from the white majority is accelerating. There is no immediate relief for the vast disparity of opportunity between the average Negro and the average white child, to which President Kennedy often referred. The gap between expectations and realities is immense, and is growing with the growing awareness of every Negro child.

It does not accomplish much to generalize about the urgency and dimensions of the racial problem. But it is necessary to be realistic about the limitations on the power of the federal government to eliminate racial discrimination by simple law enforcement. These limitations are reflected in the experience of the Department of Justice in the last few years, since it was first given any responsibility or authority in this field. Certainly they are relevant to future law enforcement once new civil rights legislation is passed. They derive from two aspects of the federal system: the control in state institutions over normally routine decisions affecting the daily lives of all citizens, and the traditional and constitutional reluctance of the federal courts to intrude. When this control is exercised without consideration of race problems, any federal-state conflicts are sporadic and haphazard. But when the issue of segregation is involved, the state controls make it everlastingly tedious, sometimes seemingly impossible, to superimpose federal standards upon the administration practiced by local institutions of government.

The danger is in the people directly affected. There exists an immense ignorance, apparently untouched by the curricula of the best universities, of the consequences of the federal system. When a violation of federal law occurs, most of those participating in civil rights work in the South (and there are thousands) think an arrest should be made by a federal officer. If there is none, and imprisonment or violence results, it is federal law and the federal government that is blamed.

A typical instance, which has happened often, might involve a student leader. He informs the Justice Department that the next day he is going to lead a group of Negroes down to register to vote in a small town in the

Deep South where no Negro has attempted to register for decades. He asks for federal protection, or at least for a show of "federal presence," in the terminology of civil rights groups. When he is told that there is no national police force, that federal marshals are only process servers working for the courts, that the protection of citizens is a matter for the local police, and that there is nothing to do until and unless something happens, the gap between his vision of government and the reality, between the expectations set forth in the Constitution and Supreme Court decisions and the hope of their fulfillment becomes too great. In the mind of the student, he has looked into the eye of federal authority, has asked the help of the federal government in exercising and realizing federal rights, and has been turned away.

The issue is framed by a contrast. On one side is the student civil rights worker just described. On the other is the established order of caste created and preserved by state institutions, which is still considered throughout most of the South to be a permanent structure of society, not strictly in the sense that there never will be any change, but rather that any change will be minimal.

These visions of the present and the future are irreconcilable. The student sees a federal right, which is immediate. The state sees either no right at all, or at worst a potential lawsuit which may in the future change its conduct to the minimum degree, affecting as few individuals of either race as possible. In the view of the state, it is legitimate and right not to move until forced to do so, and then barely to budge. It is also considered legitimate, although with somewhat less acceptance, to use the police power of the state to thwart any citizen's efforts to break the existing pattern. The states of course have the best of this struggle because all the initial decisions of the services affected—schools, parks, libraries, voter registration, and other state facilities, as well as police power—are within the control of state instrumentalities. The assertion of federal rights, on the other hand, can be realized only through the processes of the federal courts, case by case, in an endless chain of litigation.

This result has been tolerable for two reasons. First, it was accepted by Negroes as well as whites. And second, the full range of federal rights was unknown until 1954. Neither reason is now valid, and it is perfectly apparent that the result is no longer tolerable.

One consequence is the national decision that the legal right of Negroes to be free from official and systematic discrimination cannot be left to trial by combat between private citizens and the states, but must be made real through federal law enforcement. The full scope of the federal executive responsibility is being determined by the Congress. President Kennedy asked for authority to enforce all such rights, and if experience means anything, enforcement will be necessary. Since 1870, there has not been any doubt of the constitutional right of Negroes to vote, and that right has been theoretically enforceable by private suit since 1871. Yet virtually no suits were brought, and no progress was made on the problem at all in some areas, until the Justice Department was authorized to bring suit itself in 1957.

Another consequence is the testing of the durability of the federal structure as the conflict takes place. This will turn, as is true of any institution of government, on the flexibility of federalism and its ability to adapt under great strain. The system has been protected thus far, since the mid-1870s, by nonrecognition of federally guaranteed rights. This has not necessarily meant massive resistance in the sense of outright defiance of federal authority, although we have had that, but it does mean an open failure to comply with unquestioned standards of federal law until forced to do so. There is no parallel to be found in law enforcement. It is as if no taxpayer sent in a return until he personally was sued by the federal government, or no corporation respected the Sherman Act until an injunction was issued against it. The crisis is more deplorable, of course, because it is not private persons, individual or corporate, who are failing to comply with laws, but the states themselves, and the instrumentalities of state law.

A more precise way of putting the issue is: will traditional methods, largely judicial, of giving effect to federal rights work under these circumstances? An affirmative answer is the assumption of existing federal efforts, and the moderate premise of the pending civil rights bill. Is it valid? The problem is that the legal concepts have developed in terms of individual personal rights, but the rights of masses, of an entire race, are affected all at once. The solution is more within the control of the states than anywhere else. The pressures are very great, and will increase; the difficulties are serious enough that the outcome is in doubt. Some guides exist, however, in the federal experience to date in two related areas.

One is the effort to make the right to vote a reality for Negroes everywhere. This is in one sense simply a matter of law enforcement. It turns on the impact of the federal system on law enforcement action directed against state officials—a question of the ability of the federal courts to control state officials in the conduct of state business.

The other involves the effects of the rules of federal-state comity on the administration of justice in the states. State police power and criminal processes have been used in retaliation against efforts to encourage Negroes to exercise their rights to vote and to protest the caste system. They have also been used to defy or frustrate federal court orders. Manipulation of state law for either purpose involves dangerous corruption of legal institutions. For the enforcement of federal orders, of course, is essential to the ability of the federal courts to impose any federal standards at all on state instrumentalities, and the abuse of state justice for other purposes is an acute irritant to bitter race relations. The usual rules of comity against federal interference with state criminal processes were developed to avoid stresses on the federal system. Yet they have been put under such great strain by abuses for racial reasons that their survival is at issue.

The first lecture will examine the federal experience in the enforcement of voting rights, the second, in controlling abuses in the administration of justice.

☆☆

The Right to Vote

The right to vote is so often called the key to other civil rights that the phrase has become trite and suspect among civil rights groups. The United States Commission on Civil Rights, for example, went out of its way in its 1961 reports to make a study of chosen counties in Deep South states where the right to vote is freely granted, yet official racial discrimination persists, without sign of change. In the early days of President Kennedy's administration, when he and the Attorney General urged Negro leaders to concentrate on voting, they were at first met with suspicion. It was as if they were asking Negro leaders to divert their energies, and those of their organizations, into channels which would require as little change and movement as possible.

At least in the short run, it cannot be argued that securing the right to vote leads to other federal rights. It is not that easy. No significant bars to Negro voting have existed in recent years in most of Arkansas, Virginia, or North Carolina, but no more than initial steps, affecting comparatively few numbers, have been taken in any of those states.

Yet the right to vote, freely, without discrimination or harassment, is basic, as Judge John Brown of Texas recently said, because "no state, and no nation, can survive if, professing democratic rule of the governed, it flagrantly denies the voting right through racial or class discrimination." The federal system does not work at all in the areas where it is now subjected to severest strain by the race crisis, if the Negro cannot vote. If it does not bring change by itself, the vote is nonetheless the key to possible change. And most often it does make an immediate practical difference. Tennessee and Georgia are the most recent examples of the power of the Negro vote to bring about a change in political climate and atmosphere. Atlanta and Memphis, Savannah and Nashville, Richmond and Mobile, have all moved ahead of other areas of their states because the Negro vote in these cities is free and large and growing.

In any event, for this purpose it is enough that other federal rights cannot successfully be asserted where the right to vote is not protected. Only political power—not court orders or other federal law—will insure the election of fair men as sheriffs, school board members, police chiefs, mayors, county commissioners, and state officials. It is they who control the institutions which grant or deny federally guaranteed rights. The Fifth District of Georgia and the Fifth District of Mississippi have almost identical percentages of nonwhite population. The Negro population votes in the Georgia district but not, for the most part, in Southern Mississippi. The congressman from Georgia is sympathetic to the Negro cause; his colleague from Mississippi is not. That is the way the system works. Any elected official represents not the people in his district, but the people in his district who vote. When it is true, as it is only in the case of Negroes, that a large class of people are not permitted to vote, the elected officials represent only those who are opposed to Negro rights.

It was no accident that the amendment granting the right to vote explicitly to the freed slaves followed in time the Fourteenth Amendment, which granted other civil rights. The grant of political rights was considered too drastic a change when first brought up, and the proposal of the Fourteenth Amendment by Congress in 1866 followed. It was not until three years later, after the impeachment proceedings against President Andrew Johnson, and then a change in administration during which the centrifugal pull of accelerating bitterness put the Radical Republicans completely in control of the federal government, that the Fifteenth Amendment was proposed by Congress in 1869.

The right to vote thereafter was a key to Reconstruction history and the eventual capitulation of the federal government to the South, leaving the problem of the freed slaves to the control of the states in which they lived. Mississippi history, while dramatic, is not unique. In 1874, white Democrats relied on the reluctance of the federal government to continue to use military force to protect the Negro Republican vote and succeeded through arms and fear in recapturing control of state machinery for the whites. The disenfranchisement of the Negroes by terror, fraud, and deceit became complete, not only there but in the other Confederate states. Judge Chrisman of Lincoln County, Mississippi, described his state's experience in a speech to its Constitutional Convention of 1890.

Sir, it is no secret that there has not been a full vote and a fair count in Mississippi since 1875—that we have been preserving the ascendancy of the white people by revolutionary methods. In plain words, we have been stuffing ballot boxes, permitting perjury and here and there in the State carrying the elections by fraud and violence until the whole machinery for elections was about to rot down.

The convention had been called to find ways of making corruption unnecessary. As another delegate put it, there was no question but that the powers of the government were "politically and constitutionally lodged in the Negro race," and the object of the convention was to transfer it to the white race. Looking back on the Convention of 1910, at a reunion for that purpose, Mayre Dabney recalled that it "was understood in advance of the call for that Convention, that the primary purpose of it was to adopt some provision in our organic law which would secure to the State a good and stable government, freed from the incubus of Republican or negro rule from which we had suffered since the adoption of the 1869 constitution . . . some scheme . . . which would effectively remove from the sphere of politics in the State the ignorant and unpatriotic negro."

The changes in Mississippi registration laws in 1890 went far in eliminating Negro registration. What they did not do was accomplished by the invention of the white primary after the turn of the century. In other states, that device was coupled with grandfather clause enactments, requiring Negroes, but not whites, to pass stringent qualification tests for which the Negroes, as well as most whites, were largely unequipped. The Negro in the South was virtually disenfranchised. He remained so as a practical matter, and for the most part went unnoticed, North and South, until the Supreme Court outlawed the grandfather clause in 1939, and the white primary in 1944.

In most of the South, this is now a matter of history. But for significant portions of a few states, and for most of Mississippi, Negro disenfranchisement is still a current practice, almost ninety-five years after the enactment of the Fifteenth Amendment. This has been true since the removal of direct (meaning, in this case, military) federal control over the voting and registration processes, and the return of those processes to the states. Since the fall of 1960, the Department of Justice has been working intensively to eliminate racial barriers to voting through recognized methods of law enforcement by federal court litigation and injunction. No more direct federal controls have been sought. The question is whether this effort can succeed.

There would be no question, of course, if the enforcement problem was limited to the elimination of pockets of discrimination or a particular practice. But it is not. Where the problem exists at all, it is backed by a persistent determination to deny political power to the Negro.

This year we have seen the governor of one state interfere with a local registration board because too many Negroes were being registered. It was only two years ago that another state passed a whole new set of laws aimed at restricting Negro registration, and last year that a third issued new instructions for the strict use of the registration form as a kind of aptitude test.

When the will to keep Negro registration to a minimum is strong, and the routine of determining whose applications are acceptable is within the discretion of local officials, the latitude for discrimination is almost endless. The practices that can be used are virtually infinite.

It is useful, and not unfair, again to pick the state of Mississippi for illustrative purposes. National attention necessarily focuses where the resistance is deep, and an entire state cannot, even if it stood in isolation, be dismissed as an insignificant example. Further, Mississippi best shows both the shape and the dimensions of the issue. The problem it represents is not a need to create new federal rights, which was done almost a century ago, but the corruption of the federal structure when states fail to recognize the validity of existing federal rights, and instead use state instrumentalities to resist their realization.

In Mississippi then, the statistics alone are illuminating. In 1899, twenty-five years after the armed maneuvering of 1874 and nine years after the 1890 convention, the number of Negroes of voting age who were registered was down to 9 percent. By 1955, the gap had widened. In only eleven counties were over 10 percent registered (and in one of those counties the figure was to fall to less than 2 percent the following year); in eight counties, the figure was between 5 and 10 percent; in twenty counties it was from 1 to 5 percent; and in forty-three counties less than 1 percent of Negroes of voting age were registered. The total Negro registration in the state was slightly over 4 percent. These figures are approximately accurate today.

After the invalidation of the white primary, Negroes were prevented, until 1955, from registering by repeated uses of devices so absurd as to be drearily cynical. They were asked to define, for county registrars themselves without training or education, terms such as *ex post facto, habeas corpus,* due process of law, impeachment, and to interpret the preamble to the Mississippi Constitution. Some were told that they could not register until they could repeat the entire Mississippi Constitution by heart. In one county, Negro applicants were invariably informed that the registrar was not in. In another they were simply refused permission to apply at all.

The pattern of such practices had its inevitable effect. Except in a handful of counties, Negroes could not register to vote, and they did not try.

Following the school decisions of 1954, Mississippi changed its voting laws to meet the expected onslaught of federal law. These became effective on March 24, 1955. As of March, 1964, the Justice Department had brought sixteen voter registration suits in Mississippi, directly affecting twenty-two counties. Data filed by the Department in those suits, taken from records analysis in seventy-two of the eighty-two counties in the state, describe individual incidents and designs of behavior that resulted in continued Negro disenfranchisement under the new laws. Their variety exposes part of the federal law enforcement difficulty.

The records show, for instance, a wide variation in the comprehensibility of the sections of the Mississippi Constitution chosen to test applicants, a matter within the complete discretion of the registrar. For example, the simplest section used is the one stating that there shall be no imprisonment for debt. In one county, this was given often to whites, but never to Negroes. On the other hand, Negroes have been given most complex sections to explain, such as Section 236, describing in detail the levee taxes for the state.

Where the same section is used to test members of both races, the results are not fairly judged. The records disclosed repeated examples where Negroes were turned down for having given inadequate answers even though their answers were better than those given by whites who were accepted.

There were many instances, throughout the counties, of assistance being given to whites, but not to Negroes. In some counties, application forms filled out by whites consistently showed, beyond any possibility of coincidence, almost identical answers on the constitutional interpretation test. In addition, on many occasions, illiterate whites who could not read or answer the questions on the application form without help were registered after being coached by the registrar. At the same time, well-educated Negroes were turned down because of minor mistakes or because of inadequacies (in the mind of the registrar) in their answers.

Analysis of the records, coupled with interviews, also disclosed less subtle forms of discrimination. In one county Negroes, but not whites, were refused permission to apply at all unless they produced poll tax receipts. In other counties, Negroes, but not whites, were not permitted to apply to one of the deputy clerks, but instead were required to see the registrar personally, who often was unavailable. Negroes, but not whites, were refused explanation of their rejection. Negroes, but not whites, were rejected for not filling out certain blanks in the application form regarding age and prior place of residence, even though those questions were simply seeking information which appeared elsewhere on the form.

The categorization of these practices understates their effects. There is no way of meeting the discouragement that follows the rejection of a leading Negro citizen on the grounds that he is not qualified to participate in the basic act of citizenship. Timing is therefore of great importance, and it is in the matter of the passage of time that the consequences of the federal system are the most apparent.

To understand this it is necessary to see the Negro

voting problem in such counties as more than a legal issue. For it takes courage, patience, and a massive effort before a significant number of Negro residents are ready to break the pattern of their lives by attempting to register to vote. And when the effort is unsuccessful because of discrimination, delays, intimidation, or the failures of Negro applicants themselves, the promised federal rights again become illusory, and representative government in the county becomes impossible to achieve for an indefinite period.

The events in a rural Mississippi county in March, 1964, are not unusual. After weeks of preparation, and with the encouragement of clergymen from outside the state, a number of Negro citizens went to register. They stood in line outside the courthouse, in a cold rain, all day long, watched by special armed policemen, all white. The registrar permitted them to enter one at a time, unaccompanied, to be faced inside with the necessity of filling out the formidable Mississippi application form. One elderly man worked at it for over three hours; only he and perhaps the registrar can say with what agony he tried, alone and unassisted by his elected servant. The first day a total of five were processed; on the next day, which was a half-day, two applications were taken. Under Mississippi law none of the seven could know whether or not they succeeded in meeting the tests chosen by the registrar on those days. In the meantime, their names must, under state law, be published in the local newspapers, to be read by their employers and by the white community generally.

County records showed that less than 2 percent of the Negroes of voting age, and about 90 percent of the whites, were registered. By acting as rapidly as possible, the Justice Department brought suit the next week in federal court, under the 1957 civil rights act, to prevent future discrimination by the local registrar. The Department asked for, and obtained, as temporary relief, an injunction to stop a deliberate slowdown in the acceptance of applications. In addition, the complaint requested a judgment requiring the registrar to accept Negro applicants on the same basis as whites. In this fashion the federal government sought, through federal court orders, to make the ballot freely available to Negroes, starting with an order affecting the most minor detail of the operation of the registrar's office, the number of applicants to be processed each day.

Such court action begins with a fault in the federal structure which should not, but does, require federal action to mend. It could easily be corrected locally. Federal policy under Attorney General Kennedy has been to try to make the federal system in the voting field work by itself through local action, without federal court compulsion. Since the beginning of 1961 the Department has not brought a case or demanded voting records without first attempting to negotiate the matter with the local officials. The assumption has been, even when there was very good reason to believe that it was not valid, that state officials would correct any abuses which could not be defended on the facts. In this fashion, at least the substance of two continually reiterated charges is avoided. One is that federal interference is unwarranted because the states have the will and the power to correct wrongs themselves. The other is that suits are brought in the South in order to gain political advantages in the North.

Usually the negotiation is with state officials, most commonly the office of the state attorney general. The bargain is avoidance of bad publicity and the expense of a futile lawsuit in return for action to see that Negroes are freely registered, on the same basis as whites.

This has prevented bitterness and misunderstandings between state and federal lawyers. It has not in many places freed the registration processes to permit Negroes to become enrolled voters, however. For one thing, the local political situation often will not permit of any settlement between county officials and the Department of Justice, even on a nonpublic basis. The fact of Negro registration cannot be kept hidden. In addition, every county registrar is represented also by his own counsel, and local counsel are apt to stress the advantages of delay and, in some cases, the known sympathies of the local federal court.

Yet the chance of successful negotiation may also be increased by dealing directly with the local officials. In one county in southwestern Georgia, where no Negroes had been registered to vote for decades, repeated visits by a southern-born lawyer from the Department to the county board of registrars finally led to a policy decision by the board members that Negroes should be registered on the same basis as whites. More than 300 Negro citizens were registered in the county in less than two weeks. State officials never became involved at all.

In Mississippi and parts of Alabama and Louisiana, the size of the Negro population and political factors have made efforts for voluntary compliance fruitless for the most part. In these areas the political viability of white supremacy is at stake. Almost all the cases brought by the Justice Department against local registrars are concentrated in counties in these states, and they are bitterly contested. The resulting litigation comprises the single most important body of data bearing on the ability of the federal government, through the courts, to bring about an acceptance by state instrumentalities of the civil rights of Negroes under the federal constitution. The results thus far are not encouraging. A summary of the meaningful statistics relating to these suits is shown. The figures for those counties that show results are instructive.

City or County	*Date Filed*	*Percent of Negroes Registered on Filing Date*	*Percent of Negroes Registered 12/1/63*
Terrell Co., Ga.	9/4/58	1.0	4.6
Macon Co., Ala.	2/5/59	13	42
Washington Par., La.	6/29/59	4.6	23.9
Fayette Co., Tenn.	11/16/59	.73	44.2
Bienville Par., La.	6/7/60	.64	14
Bullock Co., Ala.	1/19/61	.1124	27.6
East Carroll Par., La.	4/8/61	0	4
Dallas Co., Ala.	4/13/61	1.03	1.8
Clark Co., Miss.	7/6/61	0	1.5
Forrest Co., Miss.	7/6/61	.2	1.2
Ouachita Par., La.	7/11/61	4.8	7

City or County	*Date Filed*	*Percent of Negroes Registered on Filing Date*	*Percent of Negroes Registered 12/1/63*
Jefferson Davis Co., Miss.	8/3/61	2	3.6
Montgomery Co., Ala.	8/4/61	11.3	19
Walthall Co., Miss.	8/5/61	0	.1204
Plaquemines Par., La.	10/16/61	1.5	3.3
Panola Co., Miss.	10/26/61	.014	.36
Madison Par., La.	10/26/61	0	5
Tallahatchie Co., Miss.	11/17/61	.0154	.08
Baton Rouge, La.	12/28/61	9.5	11
Jackson Par., La.	2/21/62	19	26
George Co., Miss.	4/13/62	1.2	2
Bibb Co., Ga.	5/16/62	segregated voting practices only	
Choctaw Co., Ala.	6/15/62	4	about same
Perry Co., Ala.	8/27/62	5	6
Jackson, Miss.	8/28/62	4.3	4.5
Sunflower Co., Miss.	1/26/63	.84	about same
Webster Par., La.	2/18/63	2.14	6.1
Red River Par., La.	2/18/63	1.5	3.5
Jones Co., Ga.	6/18/63	segregated voting practices only	

City or County	*Date Filed*	*Percent of Negroes Registered on Filing Date*	*Percent of Negroes Registered 12/1/63*
Hinds Co., Miss.	7/13/63	13	about same
Wilcox Co., Ala.	7/19/63	0	about same
Elmore Co., Ala.	7/19/63	6	about same
Jefferson Co., Ala.	7/31/63	9.5	15
St. Helena Par., La.	10/22/63	17	about same
West Feliciana Par., La.	10/29/63	.36	.6

Fayette County, Tennessee, apparently a spectacular success, is deceptive. The official practice attacked in that suit was a white primary, and the matter was settled by consent. The real obstacle to Negro voting in Fayette, and its neighbor, Haywood County, was not what state officials did, but massive economic retaliation by whites against Negro applicants. White businessmen and farmers, who owned the land, the banks, the stores, all the facilities needed for any normal participation in community life, combined to combat Negro voting. Their practices were attacked in federal suits. The litigation was successful, and Negroes in Fayette County, as in all Tennessee, now are free to vote without fear of reprisal. But the matter was private, not involving conflict between federal and state government.

Other substantial changes are recorded in Macon, Bullock, Montgomery, and Jefferson counties in Alabama; Washington, Bienville, and Jackson parishes in Louisiana. There are special reasons for the progress shown in each of these seven counties.

In the three parishes of Louisiana, the complaints brought by the government alleged that several years ago there had been discriminatory purges of voters already on the roll. The relief asked, and granted by the courts, was the restoration to the voting rolls of several hundreds of Negro citizens in each parish who had been wrongfully purged. This was administratively simple and immediately effective. There was no need for continued cumbersome and time-consuming court supervision of the day-to-day administration of the registration office.

In Jefferson County, Alabama (mainly the city of Birmingham), the substantial increase in Negro registration was not by reason of a court order, although the mere filing of a law-suit by the Department of Justice did affect attitudes in the county, but it was because a new board of registrars, appointed in October, 1963, decided at the outset that it was not their business to prevent Negro citizens from registering. This decision held until mid-December, 1963, when the increase in Negro registration provoked the intervention of Governor Wallace, thus making litigation inevitable.

The results of litigation in Macon, Bullock, and Montgomery counties in Alabama show that the federal courts have the power to prevent continuing racial discrimination by state officials. In each of these counties the federal court entered strong and detailed decrees against continued discrimination. Periodic reports were required on registration figures. The Justice Department asked further relief, where the reports justified it. Several times the federal judge called conferences, told the registration officials that he expected full compliance, and stated his intention to appoint federal referees under the 1960 Civil Rights Act if that proved necessary. In short, he made it plain that if racial distinctions were not eliminated by acceptance of his order, they would be eliminated through a more direct federal administration of the voting laws.

In at least two of the counties there are enough Negroes registered now that the breakthrough is inescapable, and a large Negro vote an accepted fact. But the way this was accomplished is not reassuring. It required constant, close federal judicial supervision of the registrars' conduct of their office. This is obviously an unsatisfactory resolution of federal problems. In addition, its success depends on the determination of the court to make its decrees effective. The national effort is to realize the constitutional rights of Negroes in states where they are now denied, but to do so with the smallest possible federal intrusion into the conduct of state offices, ideally by voluntary acceptance of the requirements of federal law, in the same way taxes are paid, drugs labeled, or securities regulations obeyed. This has not happened. As a result, the task rests on the federal judges, and places a heavy burden on a very few men.

The judicial selection system for federal district courts is weighted, as it should be, so that the bench reflects the customs and attitudes of the community. This is one of the facts of the federal system. At the same time, the federal judges are the only existing instruments for enforcing federal standards on state officials and for bringing about recognition of federally guaranteed rights for Negroes. The sole alternative with any precedent is the use of federal registration officials, as in the early Reconstruction period—a system which worked then only because of immediately available military force, and which ceased to work at all when that force was removed. And there are no precedents at all in other matters, such as the assignment of children to schools, the selection of juries without regard to race, or the administration of justice by police officials.

The system of selecting judges is thus a principal factor in efforts to make federal rights for Negroes a reality in the South. Even in a state where Negroes systematically have been denied the right to vote, district court appointments must have the approval of both senators from the state before the Senate will confirm them. Cases enforcing the civil rights of Negroes penetrate more deeply than any other into the society in which a judge lives and is personally a part. It is inevitable that most district judges want to do as little as possible to disturb the patterns of life and politics in their state and community. They are not reformers by profession or belief. More than one district judge has expressed hostility to federal efforts to enforce the right to vote, and others have candidly admitted their personal disagreement with the desegregation decisions of the United States Supreme Court.

These attitudes may not affect the final outcome of litigation, but they do directly and deeply affect its pace. Almost all cases brought by the Justice Department against local registrars stand in contrast to the three cases decided in the Middle District of Alabama. The first four cases filed in President Kennedy's administration were in Dallas County, Alabama; East Carroll Parish, Louisiana; and Clarke and Forrest counties, Mississippi. Each of these has been characterized by seemingly endless litigation to bring about minimal results.

Whatever the court's attitude, the suit in Forrest County shows the amount of court time and lawyer effort that may be necessary for any results. It was filed on July 6, 1961, and based in part on investigation which showed that of about 7,500 Negroes of voting age only 14 were able to register between 1949 and the spring of 1961, and none registered after 1954. The District Court refused to rule on a government request for preliminary injunction. The Court of Appeals reversed, but also issued an injunction pending appeal in March, 1962. The registrar disobeyed the injunction. On May 1, 1962, he was cited for contempt. This action had to be tried before the three judges sitting on the Court of Appeals panel and could not be set until September, 1962. It was tried for a week, briefed and finally submitted to the Court of Appeals on January 25, 1963. On July 15, approximately two years after the complaint was filed, the Court of Appeals found the registrar in civil contempt and ordered him to register 43 Negro applicants immediately and to cease other practices making Negro registration virtually impossible. The criminal contempt proceedings were held in abeyance until the Supreme Court decided whether Governor Barnett of Mississippi, the defendant in another criminal contempt case, was entitled to a jury. The civil contempt order was stayed for two months while the defendant registrar applied for review with the Supreme Court. Following that, the civil contempt order became effective. Yet subsequent examination of the treatment of Negro applicants led the government to conclude that further proceedings were necessary.

In the meantime, there has not yet been any hearing in the case on the merits. The number of Negroes of voting age who are now registered has increased to 200, over 2 percent of those in the county.

The Justice Department does not expect to win cases simply because it represents the federal government and is attempting to enforce federal rights. But there are issues at stake in this law enforcement effort which make inappropriate any analogy to other litigation or law enforcement problems. The federal system must be made to work quickly if the racial conflict is to stay within the boundaries of law. The Forrest County story does not add to anyone's confidence in the ability of his government to enforce constitutionally guaranteed voting rights effectively.

This is the danger for the future—that Negro citizens will hear only excuses when their registration efforts fail. The danger is seriously increased by the ease with which new practices aimed at restricting Negro registration can be put into effect, practices that can be stopped only by further litigation. An example is the simple device of making it almost impossible for anyone of any race to get registered in a county where most whites but no Negroes have been able to vote in the past. And it is compounded by the fact that, while the federal government has a responsibility to protect Negroes who attempt to vote, it cannot in fact guarantee fully that private citizens or local public officials will not harass them or take reprisals against them. The practices are many: cancellation of sharecropper arrangements, refusal of credit by banks and stores, a retaliatory boycott by suppliers, physical violence by a sheriff, unwarranted arrests or other police intimidation, and loss of employment. The Justice Department has filed, as of March 15, 1964, fifteen cases dealing with this problem. In one case, the Department brought suit to protect a single Negro farmer (the only Negro in his county who dared to attempt registration) from being cut off by the whites who owned the cotton-ginning equipment, the gasoline stations, and the other points of supply necessary to keep his farm in operation. In another, the Department has been litigating since June, 1962, thus far unsuccessfully, to protect a schoolteacher who was fired after her name appeared as a witness in a suit brought against the voting registrar in an adjoining county. In both cases, the will of the local Negroes to attempt to exercise their federal rights depended on the ability of the federal government to protect Negro leaders who became conspicuous.

These are examples of the obstacles to any immediate enforcement of the voting right. They are of two kinds.

One is inherent in the act of suing a state official for any purpose. The state can change the rules of the game in mid-play by amending its laws. The registrar can do the same by administrative action. He can, for example, give a difficult literacy test to everyone, without serious threat to white political supremacy if (as is common) the registration of whites, including illiterates, is already commanding, and the incidence of functional illiteracy among Negroes is high. He can always resign, and the issue is re-created. The only remedy in such a case is for the federal court to act as a substitute registrar. One federal court has reluctantly done such duty, but no federal action of that sort can result in free registration, or a lasting instrument of local government.

The other barrier is a matter of numbers, imposing on the federal court system a burden for which it was not constructed. The Justice Department has been able to protect Negro participants in registration drives from concerted economic retaliation by the white community. It is also possible to prevent reprisals against a known Negro leader, where the purpose is clear. But the firing of a maid, the threat to a janitor, the personal intimidation of individual Negroes by their white employers in counties where few Negroes have economic independence is almost beyond reach.

These difficulties can be identified, defined, and explained, one by one. They are nevertheless beyond the mass limits of credibility for most of the people affected —the Negroes who cannot vote—and to an even greater extent, young civil rights workers who have been making long efforts to bring about a change. The inability of the Justice Department to end voting discrimination quickly is attributed to a lack of effort, or will, of sufficient political motivation, and of the capacity of this form of government to meet its obligations to its citizens.

Is this a basic flaw in the federal system? The federal government has demonstrated a seeming inability to make significant advances, in seven years' time, since the 1957 law, in making the right to vote real for Negroes in Mississippi, large parts of Alabama and Louisiana, and in scattered counties in other states. Yet it is apparent that some state governments do not now function properly, and that the federal structure accordingly does not now work, because of massive denials of the right to vote. Does this mean that this basic problem is beyond solution and this simple right beyond realization?

The experience of the Justice Department to date would not justify this conclusion, and on analysis I cannot find any structural reason in federalism that it should, although I frankly set out to try. Discrimination in the registration process has been eliminated, through the normal channels of judicial action, in Macon and Bullock counties, Alabama, the heart of the Deep South. It has probably been eliminated in other places, for example,

Terrell County, Georgia, with results being not visible as yet because of the absence of effective registration efforts by local Negroes. If this has been done in these counties, failures elsewhere can be attributed not to flaws in the system, but to flaws in courts and men and to a lack of time. And these are defects that can be remedied with enough money, enough energy, enough lawyers, and enough months or years.

The harder question is whether the tempo of the civil rights movement has not quickened to such a degree that there is not enough time left. There are greater efforts now, with increasing success, to break the pattern of existence in Mississippi by mass registration drives. It can be anticipated that they will continue and, at the same time, that very few Negro applicants will be considered qualified by local registration officials. The only tangible result in the near future will be a mass of litigation in the federal courts which will take months or years to resolve. And that in itself will be divisive between Negro and white, between state and federal governments, with racial issues continuing to be a prime political factor in any election.

The gravity of the question led President Kennedy in June, 1963, to ask for legislation which would temporarily alter and temper the degree of state control over the registration process in the most difficult counties.

Under his proposal, once a suit was filed, federal officials could be authorized to begin immediately to apply state voting standards on a nondiscriminatory basis. He sought to create machinery whereby, in counties where less than 15 percent of the eligible Negroes were registered, the qualifications of Negro applicants turned down by state officials could be tested immediately, on an individual basis, but under state law, by the federal court, or its officers. There is presently no machinery provided by law, for accomplishing this.

This proposal proved unacceptable to the bipartisan consensus in the House of Representatives, and the House Judiciary Committee eliminated it from the bill. Instead, the bill passed by the House of Representatives and submitted to the Senate attempts to deal with the problem by accelerating litigation rather than changing its pattern.

The decision may prove tolerable. It shows the reluctance of the Congress as a whole, apart from racial problems, to probe beyond established state controls—even to the limited extent of permitting federal review of the judgment of state officials on the qualification of voters. But the balance of time is delicate, between an urgent need for change and the ability of whites, and their established political controls, to accept it.

There is no national sympathy with denial of the right

to vote on a racial basis, and the states or sections of states where Negro disenfranchisement is widespread are isolated, but spotlighted. The pressure for the franchise will grow, and the number of student workers and others from outside the area will increase. It is still valid that the degree of federal involvement will be determined more by the amount of acceptance of state responsibility for the recognition of federal rights, than by anything else. But the prospect for the near future is not good.

The danger is more complex than a temporary failure of law enforcement. Even if discrimination could be eradicated entirely for the future, illiteracy rates would drastically limit the number of Negro voters in Deep South counties. Yet a free Negro vote is the best chance we have for relieving the growing strain on the federal structure in those counties caused by racially motivated abuses of police power and the criminal processes of the state. As long as those practices continue, there will be increased pressures on the federal court to correct them, with lasting impact on accepted doctrines of federal-state comity. Moreover, the domestic tranquillity is at stake, for the Negro cause against discrimination is indivisible. When Negroes are excluded from participation in their government in even one county, and state authority is twisted to allow it, while federal authority appears powerless to take effective steps, the gulf between Negroes and whites everywhere is widened, and the chances of racial conflict increased. At the least, the generation of students which sees this happen are to some extent losing faith in their government, with consequences for the future that cannot be foreseen.

☆☆☆

The Administration of Justice

A necessary corollary of Negro disenfranchisement, in the limited areas where that corruption of representative government is practiced, is the double standard in favor of whites, because of their race. It is not only that qualified Negroes are rejected. Whites who are unqualified under any interpretation of state law are registered, in large numbers, solely because they are white.

What view of the impartiality of justice, of the administration of law by public officials is held by the society that countenances such practices? There is involved, for one thing, a great gap between the demands of federal law and the practices of the states. That gap is tolerated publicly, at least in home territory, on historical and constitutional grounds. But also involved is the acceptance of a double standard in the daily administration of law—in many cases clearly beyond the very large limits of permissibility set by federal constitutional standards. This double standard is presently almost outside the reach of federal action unless state criminal convictions come up for review by the United States Supreme Court. Registration and voting is basic but sporadic. A double standard of law enforcement is routine and immediate, and affects not only the citizens involved, but the concept of government held by all the public officials concerned.

An incident brought to the attention of the Justice Department in early 1961 raised the question of federal responsibility for the administration of justice by state officials. A Negro Air Force captain, accompanied by another Negro who had formerly been an officer in the Air Force, visited the home, in a large southern city, of a white major in the Air Force with whom they had done duty. A neighbor complained, and all three were arrested and charged with disturbing the peace. On the same day, in the same city, a Negro civilian employee at a nearby Air Force base was arrested and charged with disorderly conduct because he went to the home of a white co-worker to discuss official business.

There was no justification for any of the arrests, under either state or federal law. Federal employees were involved. The entire incident smacked of police-state tactics imposing segregationist rules not only on Negroes but also on individual whites who obviously did not agree with them. The only alternatives were to complain to the local authorities or to bring criminal charges against the police officers for taking action, under orders, that violated federal constitutional rights. The Justice Department took the former step, but neither course carried any real promise of changing police conduct.

What was at issue was plain abuse of police power by state officials, directed in these cases against persons who had no point to prove but who had simply acted contrary to accepted racial patterns. Quite often the citizens who are the victims of such police action are trying to prove a point, but that only aggravates the situation because the point being proved is that Negroes are the victims of a caste system. In such a case, there may be a double imposition on federal law: individual citizens are subjected to an unconstitutional exercise of police power for trying to claim constitutional rights. There are many examples, not all of them in southern counties where the vote is also denied; in most of them no direct federal action is possible, or what is attempted proves futile.

On January 8, 1963, a white student registration worker was arrested in Montgomery, Alabama, while visiting friends on a local college campus. The arrest was made by a private citizen whom the governor-elect had appointed director of Alabama's Department of Public Safety. The student was charged with conspiracy against the state, taken to jail, and interrogated. After several hours, the charge was changed to vagrancy. Bond was set at $1,000. The student was tried and found guilty within the week. He appealed, and the court ordered a new trial, but the charge was dismissed for lack of evidence. In the meantime, a new charge was placed against him—obtaining property under false pretenses. This involved a temporary lack of funds in the student's bank account, discovered only by accident because of publicity about his arrest. His trial on that charge ended with a hung jury.

On May 8, 1963, in Holmes County, Mississippi, a gasoline bomb was thrown into the home of a leading Negro citizen who had engaged in voter registration work. The next day the man and his wife were arrested and charged with arson of their own home. Four student workers who had engaged in the registration campaign also were arrested and charged with arson. One was charged, and convicted, of impeding the investigation of the arson incident by photographing the burned house. The arson charges themselves were later dismissed because there was no evidence to support the charges. The Mississippi grand jury instead indicted the local Negro and his wife for unlawful cohabitation even though they had been married for some time.

On June 18, 1963, in Itta Bena, Mississippi, fifty-seven Negroes were arrested on charges of disturbing the peace, after they had made a night march to the home of a deputy sheriff to ask police protection for their voter registration work. The next day, every one of the fifty-seven over fourteen years old was tried in a group (there were four groups in all), found guilty, and sentenced. All four trials were completed in slightly over one hour. Each man was sentenced to six months in jail and a $500 fine. Each woman was sentenced to four months and a $200 fine. They were not represented by counsel. There was no evidence specifically linking any identified individuals to any particular disorderly acts.

On August 6, 1963, three Negro student workers were arrested in Ruleville, Mississippi, for accompanying would-be Negro voters to the polls, and asking local officials about voting procedures. The mayor, in his capacity as chief of police, ordered the arrests. The students were charged, under a loosely worded Mississippi statute, with attempting to commit an offense. They were taken to the town hall and tried by the mayor in his capacity as magistrate. They were convicted, and sentenced to thirty days in jail and fined $100 each. At the trial the mayor commented that "everyone" knew what had happened, and that there was no need to take any testimony.

On August 8, 1963, four student workers were arrested in Americus, Georgia, and charged, among other things, with insurrection, a capital offense under Georgia law. The students had been involved, two of them only indirectly, in local demonstrations protesting segregation. They were held, without bond, until January, 1964, when a federal court ruled the statute was unconstitutional. Back in October (after the students already had been held without bail for several weeks) the local prosecuting attorney had stated that he "frankly" seriously doubted whether he would ever call the cases up for trial. "The basic reason for bringing these charges," he said, "was to deny the defendants, or ask the court to deny them bond."

On September 19, 1963, twelve Negro citizens of Clinton, Louisiana, wrote letters to the mayor and district attorney respectfully requesting the creation of a biracial committee on community relations "in order to avoid civil domestic disturbances of racial tension." The Negroes suggested that a committee made up of both races could give "careful consideration of the many problems facing our community." On December 3, all twelve persons were arrested on charges of intimidating public officials. Each was required to post bond of $4,000. One of those arrested was a woman seventy-five years old who had lived in the area all her life. Another was the husband of the superintendent of the Negro schools in the parish.

On September 22, 1963, a Negro walked down a street in Clarksdale, Mississippi, wearing a T shirt with the inscription "CORE" on the front and "Freedom Now" on the back. He was arrested and charged with parading without a permit. On subsequent days, other Negro students were similarly treated.

Later in the fall of 1963 in Selma, Alabama, a sixteen-year-old boy was arrested for unlawful assembly after carrying a sign in front of a drugstore. He was released from jail when a relative signed a statement that he would not participate in any demonstrations for a year. His activity in front of the drugstore was observed by three policemen for fifteen to twenty minutes, without incident, prior to the arrest. A large number of other officers of the police Department were near at hand. The sign said: "Don't buy where you can't eat. Register to vote."

These examples cannot be disposed of as sporadic abuses

of official power by minor bureaucrats. In each case, the official action was taken by leading citizens of the community. The incidents received wide attention throughout their communities and were defended by the local newspapers. Some cases attracted national interest for a time.

Since 1960, such incidents have been multiplied by hundreds of constitutionally dubious arrests in sit-in incidents and massive denials of First Amendments rights following demonstrations protesting segregation policies. In many cases, however, the constitutional limits on police action were sufficiently vague, or so much in flux at the time that no implication of deliberate double standard is provable.

This has led in the past three years to the greatest single source of frustration with and misunderstanding of the federal government, particularly among young people. They cannot understand federal inaction in the face of what they consider, often quite correctly, as official wholesale local interference with the exercise of federal constitutional rights. Apparently their schools and universities have not taught them much about the working of the federal system. In their eyes the matter is simple. Local authorities are depriving certain people of their federal rights, often in the presence of federal officials from the

Justice Department. Persons doing this should be protected.

What is wrong with this analysis? Is the federal government simply failing to meet a clear responsibility for enforcing federal law?

The question embraces all the deepest complexities of the federal system. It is surrounded by some basic constitutional notions which have worked, and worked well, in other contexts, preserving the dilution of powers intended by the framers of the Constitution, and at the same time protecting individuals against deprivation of their freedoms.

The most fundamental, primary notion, of course, is that the constitutional rights involved are individual and personal, to be asserted by private citizens as they choose, in court, speaking through their chosen counsel. If the matter is one of unjustified criminal charges, the individual's rights are protected by the court system and by the right of trial by jury. If an unjust or unconstitutional conviction is obtained, it can be appealed. If the federal system of justice is not recognized and followed by the state courts, then recourse is had from review by the United States Supreme Court or in the federal courts through *habeas corpus*. In this fashion individual rights are protected on an individual case-by-case basis, as they should be. All that is involved is a question of time. Even that is not of major importance as long as reasonable bail is allowed while the questions are in litigation.

Two other fundamental concepts flow from this structure of protecting federal rights. One is that rights must be asserted by individuals. The other is that federal courts will not interfere while the system is at work—that is, they will not enjoin a *pending* or *future* state criminal proceeding.

In general the first of these concepts means that federal government itself has no right to bring suit in federal court to protect federal rights guaranteed to individuals. For most of our history, this has not been a matter of debate. The fact of *en masse* deprival of rights has been limited, for various reasons, to Negroes. The principal one is that they are the only Americans who have been lumped together everlastingly by race into a solid caste openly treated differently from everyone else by law, and not recognized as individuals, in one significant section of the nation. Indeed, from 1896 to 1954 the system had a sort of sanction in federal law as well, under the myth that a society based on white supremacy would provide equal, if separate, schools and other facilities for the

Negro. Again, for various reasons including mainly the denial of the right to vote, discrimination against Negroes has been largely ignored by most whites until very recently.

Recently this particular deference to the states has been under attack. A Supreme Court decision in 1894, justifying federal intervention against union activity tying up railroad facilities, appears to furnish some basis for federal legal action where federally protected interests are at stake. A three-judge court in Louisiana recently said that where the complaint "is based on a state law which is contrary to the superior authority of the United States Constitution, the Nation, as well as the aggrieved individuals, is injured." In technical terms, this would mean that the United States, through the Department of Justice, would have standing to sue to attack statutes presumptively used on a large-scale basis to deny to individuals their constitutional rights.

This is a matter of speculation. The opinion decided a case attacking Louisiana voting laws. It was brought under the 1957 Civil Rights Act which was expressly intended to give the United States standing to bring suit to prevent denials of voting rights. The Congress has thus far refused to pass a statute to authorize the Justice

Department, in a broad sense, to seek injunctions in federal courts to prevent any denial by state officials of federally protected rights, although parts of the pending Civil Rights Bill would give the Department standing to attack school segregation, and discrimination in other municipal facilities such as parks and playgrounds. Other decisions disagree with the one in Louisiana.

In any event, under existing law, federal courts strongly resist interfering with state court criminal proceedings. An individual suit asking such relief is barred by statute for most purposes. Attempts to change the pattern of federal restraint have not worked. The language of constitutional law is full of tributes to the delicate balance of federal-state relations in criminal law matters. Some of the most intricate and important differences of opinion in the Supreme Court have turned on related questions.

Thus more is at issue than whether the federal government has any responsibility at all, at least in court, to try to prevent unconstitutional state police action. In the entire course of our federal legal history, there has been but a handful of occasions where a federal court enjoined a state from prosecuting criminal charges for any reason. In most of those, the court has acted to protect one of two overriding, sometimes complementary, interests: enforcing its own orders, or preventing use of an unconstitutional criminal statute. Only once has a federal court issued an injunction to prevent unadorned abuse of police power, a case turning on the special statutory interest of the United States in preventing intimidation of citizens seeking to vote in federal elections.

The case arose in Tylertown, Mississippi, in 1961. A young Negro registration worker brought two or three applicants to the county clerk's office to apply. No Negro in the county was registered to vote at the time. The registrar flatly refused to accept the applications, and attacked the student worker with a pistol, hitting him twice on the head. The student fled and found the sheriff, who arrested the student on charges of disorderly conduct. The case was set for trial. The Justice Department filed suit immediately in federal court, charging intimidation of Negro applicants for voter registration, and asking for a temporary injunction against the prosecution of the student worker. When that was refused, within a few hours application for a stay was made to the federal appellate court. The matter was expedited, and an agreement not to prosecute pending decision arranged with the state. The appellate court sometime later ordered a preliminary injunction granted.

The argument presented by the United States was that its interest could not otherwise be protected, except by injunction against prosecution of the student worker. But its interest was not in the student's constitutional rights. It was assumed in the litigation, and necessarily so, that his rights would be protected by the normal processes of the state court system, with ultimate review in the federal courts if a federal constitutional issue was raised.

The government instead claimed an interest because the student's prosecution, even if unsuccessful, would have a bad effect on efforts by Negroes in the county to register. The Justice Department contended that the only purpose of the prosecution was to intimidate potential Negro applicants by the mere fact of prosecution in a rural Mississippi county, making it necessary to employ personal counsel (actually unavailable), post bail, and to meet other consequences of defending a criminal suit.

The argument succeeded because the facts were so telling. In similar suits brought by the Department of Justice, they have not been so clear-cut. Either there has been a possibility of other relief, or the time for action has been too short; at any rate the federal court has refused to interfere, leaving the government, and the personal constitutional rights of the individuals affected, to such protection as is available under the legal (not factual) assumption that the complex state-federal court systems will end up protecting federal as well as state interests.

The civil rights movement and public protests against segregation and racial discrimination have put a strain on these assumptions and rules of federal-state comity that is far greater than it has ever been. The massive number of arrests in the past four years is one factor. Another is the amount of bail required, making unreal the supposition that anyone convicted of a state crime can be free while the legality of his conviction under federal law is being tested. But the greatest impetus is from the immediacy and urgency of the protest movement, whose members do not understand their rights, vastly overestimate the scope of the First Amendment, and in large part do not care. These factors converge as part of the forces pulling towards a polarization between Negro leaders and their government, causing a loss in faith among young people that the federal government has the ability or will to protect constitutional rights in the South, and fostering the belief that gains can be made only through continued protest demonstrations in the streets, creating, as the Reverend Martin Luther King,

Jr., has put it, a situation of total crisis which cannot be escaped.

Does this mean that the rules of comity, of federal tolerance of the administration of justice by states, should be reexamined? The concepts are not, after all, unalterable. At least two modes of basic change have been proposed: one to enable the Department of Justice to seek federal court injunctions against any deprivations of federally protected rights; and the other to permit removal to the federal courts of any trials claimed to infringe constitutional guarantees. The second proposal has many difficulties: it would require a federal court to decide in advance when the state system will not work; it conceives of the federal judge as presiding over state law enforcement proceedings; it assumes a fairness in federal judges and federal juries above that available in state courts; and it ignores the administrative burden that would be thrust upon an overloaded federal judiciary unprepared for new strains. Nevertheless, that proposal in essence contemplates no more than a change in the forum of trial. The first envisages no trial at all, and cuts—as will be seen—much more deeply into the law enforcement structure of the nation. Yet both are legally conceivable, and have been vigorously advanced. In short, the insulation of state criminal processes from federal interference is not itself required by the Constitution. Should it be eliminated, or at least penetrated and changed?

It is difficult for anyone concerned with corruption of the law to say corrections are not needed. Negro disenfranchisement over decades has created a system of all-white courts, staffed entirely by white officials. The apparent inability of the bar to bring itself to provide counsel in cases involving racial implications is alone one proof that our basic assumptions about the workings of justice in state courts are wrong. The unavailability of normal sources of bail is another. Examples of abuse of authority such as I have cited are a third. They are compounded by repeated exclusion of Negroes from juries, enforced segregation and racial abuses in courtrooms, and other evidences of the weight of state authority thrusting imbalance into the processes of justice where racial customs are threatened.

All of this is, as the Civil Rights Commission has said, an affront to the conscience of the nation. Such inequity cannot be tolerated indefinitely in a free society. The question facing President Kennedy in June, 1963, and still confronting the country today, is whether it warrants or requires, as many have agreed, fundamental alterations in the relationships between the state and the federal courts, in the administration of justice.

The complete consequences of even limited adjustments of this sort can be seen only after years of experience. Some are inevitable, however, and can at least be identified and described.

For one thing, constitutional rights are indivisible. They cannot be segmented to deal with a particular problem, even that of race. The frustration and fury at state-controlled administration of justice is directed, first, at the resistance in southern states to the constitutional outlawing of official segregation by the Supreme Court, and secondly at the suppression of protests directed against the unofficial caste system in employment practices and public places which accompanied official segregation. But the personal constitutional rights affected are the rights to the equal protection of the laws, and to freedom of speech.

The wrongs are limited geographically, are hopefully transitional, and are in any event capable of definition. None of this is true of the constitutionally protected rights which would be affected by adjustments in the rules of comity presently controlling federal-state relations. If the federal courts are to be granted general powers to prevent state prosecutions from depriving a defendant of rights granted under the Fourteenth Amendment, those powers will not be limited to enjoining the prosecution of student civil rights workers in Georgia under that state's insurrection statute. They would include, among others in a wide range, power to stop criminal proceedings where a constitutional issue is raised as to the conduct of the trial (such as lack of counsel or racial bias in jury selection), and power to prevent prosecutions where claims are made under the First Amendment (such as censorship and interference with freedom of religion or speech).

So basic a change in the administration of the federal-state court systems would have such a clearly foreseeable impact on the speedy processing of criminal justice in the state courts that it has always met with deserved resistance. As the system now works, federal constitutional issues are tested after trial and conviction, upon the basis of the record at the trial. They are tested in the first instance in the state court. To permit them to be tested prior to trial in the federal courts, based upon a record which would be different than the record of the criminal proceedings in the state court, would permit defendants to delay their prosecution indefinitely. Furthermore these effects cannot be limited to matters arising from the distortions of the federal system linked to the civil rights crisis. It is too easy to raise at least a substantial question of a constitutional claim. The prospect of this litigation in the federal courts, prior to state trial, is by itself such a disadvantage that if there is a solution, it should be sought elsewhere.

These are purely administrative difficulties, however. There is a more fundamental objection to the suggestion that the Attorney General be given power to seek federal court injunctions against general denials of constitutional rights to individuals. There is no way of depriving him then of the power of choice. If the full range of constitutional rights were to be protected in this fashion, the Attorney General would have the power of choosing among them. He could decide either to use the resources and power of the Justice Department to protect economic rights, or not. He could at his will enter or avoid the field of censorship. He could defend or ignore plain deprivation of religious rights, including all of the rights of children in public schools. Within each of these fields, the powers of choice would be immense.

It is no answer to say that the Attorney General always has had the power to decide what cases to bring. It is one thing to make decisions in enforcing tax laws, or even to choose between conflicting economic considerations in enforcing antitrust statutes. It is another to give the government choices in advancing or protecting human rights. Decisions in protecting all constitutional rights demand choices among religions, or between religions and atheism. They permit choices among political movements, between integrationists and segregationists, between peace marchers and militarists—among, in short, all competing views as to the proper future course of the United States and of mankind.

Such problems, of course, are the result of the breadth of what has been suggested. Some of them can be eliminated or at least narrowed in scope, to cut back on the practical possibility of any real danger to the society. There would yet remain a matter of power, the physical power of law enforcement and the responsibility for keeping order, which could not be avoided by draftsmanship or lawyers' work. It derives from interrelationship between the administration of justice in state courts and the use of police power in the streets. It is unavoidable.

A fair test of whether the problem of abuse of police power and criminal prosecution in the states can be dealt with directly at all under the federal system is to assume that a statute could be so drawn as to give the Attorney

General the power to enjoin interference with constitutionally protected protests against racial injustices, and to do nothing else. That is, after all, the heart of the matter. What would be the consequences of that limited a use of the federal courts to prevent arrests and criminal prosecution that are, in any event, constitutionally prohibited?

A vivid piece of recent history suggests the answer. This was the sequence of events that took place in Alabama and Mississippi during the Freedom Rides of May, 1961.

In December, 1960, the Supreme Court decided that passengers using interstate bus lines had a federal right to be free from racial discrimination in bus terminals. The Freedom Rides followed to test whether this federal right was truly recognized in southern terminals. The rides were scheduled to end in New Orleans on May 17, the anniversary of the school cases of 1954, traversing on the way Virginia, North Carolina, South Carolina, Georgia, Alabama, and Mississippi.

The trip proceeded without attracting national attention to Atlanta, Georgia, where the riders divided into two groups, one traveling by Greyhound, and the other by Trailways, to Birmingham, Alabama, on May 14. The

Greyhound bus was attacked in Anniston, Alabama, by a gang of men carrying clubs, chains, and blackjacks. They broke windows, slashed tires, and burned the bus. The Trailways bus was met at the Birmingham station by other men who severely beat several members of the Freedom Ride group. Birmingham police did not arrive until several minutes after the violence occurred, although the scheduled arrival of the bus had been well publicized, and was observed by a number of newsmen.

During the next week, President Kennedy and the Attorney General attempted to persuade Governor Patterson of Alabama and local authorities to accept the police responsibility for the safety of the buses and the passengers. Until assurances of protection could be obtained, it was impossible to find a bus driver who was willing to take the bus to Montgomery, its next scheduled stop. In the meantime, the original group of Freedom Riders had been replaced by others who sat each day in buses at the Birmingham terminal waiting to be taken to Montgomery. Governor Patterson was at first unavailable, even to the President. Finally, on Friday, May 20, the governor agreed to see a representative of the President from the Justice Department.

He gave assurances that he had the will, the force, the

men, and the equipment to protect everyone in Alabama, including interstate travelers.

On Saturday, May 21, a Greyhound bus carrying a Freedom Ride group proceeded from Birmingham to Montgomery under escort of Alabama State Police. The bus was met in Montgomery by another mob of about 1,000 persons who rioted and attacked the group of riders, beating them with pipes, sticks, clubs, and fists. The President's representative who had met with Governor Patterson was himself struck down while attempting to assist one of the Freedom Riders, a girl, to escape the mob. He lay on the sidewalk for twenty-five minutes before police took him to a hospital. A federal court later found that the Montgomery police had engaged in willful and deliberate failure to provide protection before or after the bus had arrived.

As the situation developed during the week, the Department of Justice made plans for federal action in the event that state authorities continued to fail to protect American citizens traveling interstate and seeking to exercise federal rights despite local resentment. When state and local authorities failed to protect the Freedom Riders in Montgomery, despite the assurances given by Governor Patterson, these plans were put into effect. On Saturday, the Department sought and obtained a restraining order from the federal court in Montgomery against Ku Klux Klan groups involved in the violence to prevent their continued interference with interstate travel. The Department also sought and obtained an order preventing the Montgomery police from continuing to fail to provide protection for interstate travelers.

In this way the groundwork was laid for the use of direct federal police action to enforce the court order. Some 600 federal officers from the Border Patrol, the Bureau of Prisons, the Alcohol and Tobacco Tax Unit of the Treasury, and various United States marshals' offices in a number of states, all of whom had been on an alert since the previous Thursday, were instructed to proceed to Montgomery, where they were sworn in as deputy marshals for the Middle District of Alabama. The men were put under orders from the then Deputy Attorney General, Byron White, whose instructions were to assist state and local officials in seeing that the orders of the federal court were complied with and that the laws of the United States were executed. The entire plan was based upon the President's instructions to the Attorney General to take such measures as were necessary to suppress domestic violence, and protect the right of citizens of the United States to travel among the states.

On Sunday night, May 21, and the early morning of May 22, the deputized marshals were required to perform police duty to protect a Negro church in which Martin Luther King, Jr., was holding a mass meeting. A large mob gathered outside the church, burned a car in the area, and advanced upon the church throwing rocks and bottles. The mob was broken up by the federal officers with tear gas and billy clubs, and a disaster was prevented. Control was finally established when the local police arrived and joined forces with the federal agents, and after Governor Patterson put Montgomery under martial law and called out the National Guard. The federal agents went on duty at the church at about 6 o'clock Sunday evening and were withdrawn about 2 A.M. Monday. During the day a few had been placed at bus terminals to see that interstate travelers were not mobbed.

The Freedom Riders were determined, as was their right, to proceed from Montgomery to Jackson, Mississippi, by bus, and then on to New Orleans. The Attorney General asked that order be preserved by state and local authorities in Mississippi and received assurances from Governor Barnett and Mayor Thompson of Jackson. It had to be decided whether to accept the word of these officials in view of events in Montgomery following the assurances given by Governor Patterson. There was considerable evidence that there would be violence in Mississippi. Nevertheless, it was doubtful whether the President had any constitutional choice about refusing in advance to accept the word of the governor of a state, and it was clearly necessary in any event to try immediately to re-establish the responsibility of the states to use their constitutional police powers to maintain order. The federal decision was made on that basis. The bus was completely unaccompanied by any federal officials when it proceeded from Montgomery to the Alabama border under escort of Alabama officials and when it traveled across Mississippi to Jackson, it was guarded solely by the Mississippi Highway Patrol.

In Jackson, order was maintained, but federal law was not. The Freedom Riders were arrested when they attempted to use the bus terminal facilities on an integrated basis. The constitutionality of those arrests is still, almost three years later, undetermined. Conviction of one of the Riders was recently affirmed by the Supreme Court of Mississippi on the grounds that the defendant came to Jackson for the deliberate purpose of inciting violence, even though the violence incited was from local whites who resented his efforts to exercise his federal right to be free from racial discrimination in the Jackson bus terminal. During the summer that followed, a large number of Negro and white citizens who traveled to Jackson and attempted to use bus terminal facilities on an integrated basis were also arrested and jailed. Efforts to obtain federal court orders to enjoin these arrests were unsuccessful.

The constitutional and doctrinal basis for the use of federal deputy marshals in Montgomery is sufficiently complex to justify a set of lectures by itself. The incident resulted in a coalescing of the functions of state and federal governments with the responsibilities of each unclear for a period of time. The chief of police at Montgomery asked, when federal officials started arriving early Sunday morning, whether they intended to take over the traffic and fire control duties in the city. His remark shows the dilemma which the federal system imposes on the nation when a clash between federal and local law, and federal and local standards, is so deep on a substantive issue that the police machinery of the state is not available to perform its proper function.

In effect, in Anniston, in Birmingham, and in Montgomery, the white people and the authorities of Alabama tried to deal with the problem of federal rights which they found unacceptable by abdicating police responsibility. The expectation was that the matter would be resolved, as Reconstruction was finally resolved, and as the entrance of a Negro girl into the University of Alabama in 1956 had been resolved, by terror and violence which the federal government would not stop. Federal rights were protected finally only because the federal government did act, at the cost of a temporary and localized, though constitutionally permitted, alteration of the federal system as it usually operates, with federal police performing functions that were the responsibility of the state.

In Mississippi, in contrast, the state authorities met their police responsibilities, but preserved order by refusing to give any effect in their police action to the federally protected rights that were at issue. Their assumption apparently was that the time consumed between arrest and the final vindication of federal rights by the United States Supreme Court, the amount of bail required, the unavailability of counsel, and the other delays and imperfections in the constitutional mechanics of protecting federal rights in state criminal proceedings would prove so discouraging that the federal rights would atrophy. It was for this reason that the city of Jackson tried every case separately. This was done even though the facts did not vary and the legal issues could have been tested in a single case. Accordingly, every Freedom Rider who had gone to Jackson during the spring and summer had to retain a lawyer, put up bail, and return for trial in an endless procession.

The acceptance by the federal government of a responsibility directly to protect persons exercising federal rights in Alabama when the state failed to do so had wide implications. Failure to take action was unjustified then and intolerable in the long run. Other Freedom Rides would have followed at best, simply creating a new situation with each day. At worst, federal authorities would have permitted state inaction and mob violence to inhibit or destroy the willingness of Negroes to exercise federally protected rights. The action that was taken unquestionably led to a renewed acceptance of responsibility for order by both the states of Alabama and Mississippi.

On the other hand, what happened in Mississippi was not satisfactory. Persons going to Missisippi to exercise federal rights were arrested. Many were jailed; others had to meet a heavy burden of raising cash bonds and litigating their causes. The federal courts refused to enjoin the arrests. Should the system of law which permits this result be allowed to continue?

It would be possible to devise authority for the federal

courts to enjoin such arrests. There ie no constitutional or doctrinal difficulty involved. But the consequences would be to destroy the means by which Mississippi maintained order. An injunction could be justified as a matter of equity and under the constitution against the city authorities to prohibit arrests of persons protesting interference with the use of the bus terminal facilities on an integrated basis. What would be the practical effect?

The sequence of events in Mississippi and Alabama strongly suggests that the result would have been chaotic and more destructive of the federal system than what happened in Mississippi. The assurances given by Governor Barnett and the Mississippi authorities were based on the assumption that the police could arrest the demonstrators rather than control the mob. It is doubful that they could have been obtained had it been clear that the arrests would be prohibited.

The issue at least can be stated clearly. On the one hand, state police thought, or were told by their lawyers, that they could arrest any Negro or mixed group attempting to use a white waiting room, and charge them with disturbing the peace, or inciting to riot, or other local offenses. The arrests might be wrong, but that is not the question. The question is whether a federal court should be empowered in advance to decide they are unlawful, and to use its process to prevent them. If that is done, what is the order that the court issues? How large a crowd should be permitted to gather before police action is permissable, under the court decision? What is constitutional in a town with almost no police, and what in a city if the police stay home? Who will advocate the federal police force that would be necessary if these decisions had to be made within minutes or, at the most, hours? The questions are easier to answer in theory than by those having responsibility for the domestic tranquillity. They are less debatable where the rights are clearly defined than where demonstrations and the defensible limits of protest are at stake.

It may be said that these difficulties are a result of the existence of federal rights, and the requirements of the constitution. They are nonetheless what would have to be faced, and are not faced under the accepted roles of the federal and state governments under any existing legislation, or by the supporters of direct federal court control over police action. The deputy marshals in Montgomery were drawn from various federal agencies, assigned on a temporary basis, and could not possibly have operated for any extended period of time to maintain order in the city. There are no available federal police resources, and their use would not be tolerable over a period of time in any event. The dilemma is in this sense insoluble. There is no satisfactory way to prevent police interference with the exercise of federally protected rights under such circumstances. And it should be noted that this is not necessarily a loss to our national interest. The time spent under the federal system in protecting the rights of demonstrators under law performs a function of its own by creating a period in which to attack directly the substantive problem of discrimination (in this case segregation in the bus terminal) instead of attempting to prevent the police from interfering with demonstrations protesting the discrimination.

This is what happened finally in Jackson, and elsewhere in Mississippi.

Eventually federal court orders enjoined the police and city authorities from maintaining segregation in terminals, on the same basis as an injunction against segregation in schools or other public facilities. Official segregation signs in front of the terminals were removed. There were hours of crisis, particularly in McComb, Mississippi, when the need for direct federal intervention to protect persons availing themselves of a court order hung in the balance. But in the end the local authorities in McComb and other cities met their responsibilities. No direct federal interference with the police function as such was necessary, and the question of law enforcement that remained was the more general one of the ability of the federal courts to change the structure of Alabama and Mississippi society through injunctions against official racial discrimination.

For the present, this solution has worked. Persuasion, or federal legal pressure, or changes in local law in one way or another has resulted in accommodations, quickly enough, in particular places, to the driving need for racial fairness and some equality of treatment. For the reasons just discussed, it is fortunate that this is so. We are still at the edges of the legal problem of equality under law in most of the southern states. Yet official discrimination has become barely tolerable over the shortest period. Many of the current methods of public protest against racial injustice are not constitutionally protected, but neither are many of the repressive police tactics taken in retaliation. There are controls over the violations of local law, but only delayed, legalistic, theoretical restraints on police.

Under these circumstances, how long will the inescapable dilemma of the federal system continue to permit resistance to demands for direct federal controls over local police action? There are several factors at work.

A principal one, as in any federal-state conflict, is the future conduct of state officials, as the requirements of federal law become clearer. It has been possible for city attorneys and other lawyers for police officials in recent months to rely on lack of clarity in the federal law. After all, there are many Supreme Court decisions on freedom of expression and the right of protest, and over a period of time the opinions have not been unanimous, or capable of resolution into a simple set of rules. The number of people who must be allowed to picket, the places and times that are protected, the constitutionality of requiring a permit are all matters open to debate. Even in the case of individual arrests, apparently without conceivable justification, some issue can be created.

As the protests against racial discrimination have increased, these ambiguities decrease. The Supreme Court has been required to decide more and more cases arising from official repression of assertions of racial equality. The Court's recent decisions overturning mass arrests of racial demonstrators in South Carolina are one example.

Its summary reversal of a contempt citation of a Negro woman who refused to answer questions put to her when addressed by her first name is another. The Court has already defined at least some limitations on the power of police to make arrests in sit-in cases, where the state participated in racial discrimination by privately owned business. There are other cases pending now which will establish what further limitations, if any, exist.

The point is not to analyze the decisions themselves. It is enough that they are being made, inescapably, by reason of the function of the Court, and that once made, they clarify federal law, the rights of the people, and the constitutional limitations on the power of the police. To the extent these decisions are ignored by police officials, as the school decisions of 1954 have been ignored by most school boards in eleven states, cynicism, distrust of government, and disbelief in any kind of law will increase. So will the inescapable pressures for federal control of local police, by court injunction or otherwise.

Recent events in various southern towns suggest that the danger of overwhelming abuses of police authority will be overcome by local restraint and experience. The idea of racial protest was unthinkable, only months ago, in many places, and the first who protested suffered accordingly. In at least some cities, this was caused by bad legal advice, or none, and by inexperience. The area of total resistance to any protest has in any event become limited.

The important factor, however, is not the question of abuse of police authority as such. Our national objective is not to protect the First Amendment right to protest racial discrimination, but to end the discrimination itself. This is the purpose of the pending bill. It assumes, as do the present voting laws, that this purpose can be accomplished, under law, through the processes of the federal courts, and without further federal interference with local police, educational, or other functions. The main issue is whether that effort can succeed.

In part, this turns on the ability of the federal government to see to it that court orders are enforced. The technical side of the question has been resolved wherever it has arisen. In the fast-moving litigation arising from state interference with the admission of James Meredith to the University of Mississippi, the federal courts enjoined the prosecution of a criminal action against Meredith; his arrest on a conviction from a state criminal trial *in absentia* the day before his enrollment; any further proceedings in a civil action in state court to prevent his enrollment; and the enforcement of a newly enacted

Mississippi law to make his entrance into the university a state crime. Legally parallel injunctions were issued against enforcement of state laws passed in Louisiana directed against the New Orleans school board in 1960 and 1961. These results are examples of the quick erosion the rules of federal-state comity may undergo under severe threat by state defiance of federal law.

The dangerous aspect of the cases is the notion of perpetual relitigation of issues, on the grounds that some court may change its mind. After the Meredith case, the charge was made that the riots at Oxford were "precipitated by the unwillingness of Attorney General Kennedy to await the completion of judicial processes," and that pending court matters were "interrupted by the use of armed marshals and troops with resulting death, injury, destruction to property and expense to the taxpayers." The basis for the charge, in legal theory, was that Governor Barnett's interposition of himself, and the state sovereignty, between the federal government and the university required a new legal testing of Meredith's qualifications to enter the university, of the validity of the school decisions of 1954 and before, and of concepts of state sovereignty and the doctrine of interposition which would cut into deeply embedded roots of our society.

By itself, the Oxford riot was an isolated incident in

which the President had no choice once he had exhausted, as he did, every effort to persuade and permit the state authorities to meet their responsibilities. The idea that no legal issue is ever foreclosed, that every rule of law and every contest of fact can in some fashion be kept open to change, was put forward to justify a governor's actions. If that were the end of the matter, there would be no great concern for the country.

The difficulty is—and it is a major one—that once the notion is accepted that everyone can retest basic constitutional decisions, no one obeys the law. This is what endangers the authority of local and state police in the long run. They may decide, in the pattern of massive resistance, to continue to ignore the requirements of federal law until their actions go beyond the limits of tolerance by the nation at large. This attitude already has resulted in long-overdue federal executive intervention in voting rights in the Civil Rights Acts of 1957 and 1960. Those statutes would not have been enacted had not the states where voting discrimination exists failed to take any steps to eliminate it, until the federal government was authorized to step in and sue each registrar. The school provisions of the pending legislation became inevitable because as a result of massive resistance, compliance with the school decisions of 1954 has slowed to a point where none can be expected in large sections of the country without federal court orders, district by district, in painful detail.

Those who say that civil rights issues cut into the fabric of federalism are correct. They cut most deeply where police power is involved, for the police as well as for those in conflict with the police. There would be vast problems in any attempts at federal control of the administration of justice, even through the moderate method of federal court injunctions. Yet vast problems have been created already by police indifference to Negro rights in the South, and they will grow if the trend is not turned. The loss of faith in law—the usefulness of federal law and the fairness of local law—is gaining very rapidly among Negro and white civil rights workers. The consequences in the future cannot be foreseen.

☆☆☆☆

Conclusion

At the beginning of these lectures, I referred to the expanding dimensions of President Kennedy's decision to ask a total national commitment to ending official or systematic racial discrimination.

The aspects of federalism I have described illuminate some of those dimensions. They create the need for new legislation. At the same time they illustrate the difficulties of enforcement which unavoidably flow from dependence on federal court injunctions to protect federal rights, and which new legislation will bring. The passage of the pending civil rights bill thus will lead the nation to a new time of decision, shared by millions of citizens, of whether the law of the land is to be accepted. If there is not wide compliance, the consequences of the federal system will create great frustrations and the structure of the nation will suffer.

The essence of what is happening is a reversal of history. Between 1875 and 1885 federal prohibitions against racial discrimination were withdrawn or became ineffective. The principal federal statute was struck down in 1883. During the next decade federal standards were replaced by state laws establishing the caste system. These set the pattern of society in many states and still do. Yet ten years ago the process of reassertion of federal constitutional policy over state law was completed by the school segregation decisions. The law was made clear, but there was no general compliance. Now it is necessary to create again, by statute, federal rights and federal remedies, in a new effort to rid the nation of discriminatory practices.

What happened following Reconstruction took place under law, in part as a result of court decisions. The consequences were clearly foreseen, at the time, in the dissents of Justice John Marshall Harlan. His words foretold the history that followed. There is no better capsule statement of how the problems grew up, problems which confront us now in a national crisis.

In 1883, the Supreme Court held the Civil Rights Act of 1875 to be beyond the power of Congress to enact. Justice Harlan said that if Congress could not "independently of the action or non-action of the States" legislate to protect federal rights, if that obligation "rested primarily, not on the nation, but on the States," then

not only the foundations upon which the national supremacy has always securely rested will be materially disturbed, but we shall enter upon an era of constitutional law, when the rights of freedom and American citizenship cannot receive from the nation that efficient protection which heretofore was unhesitatingly accorded to slavery and the rights of the master.

Then in 1896, the Court upheld the theory of separate but equal state facilities for Negro citizens. It was in his dissent to that opinion that Justice Harlan used the phrase "our Constitution is color-blind." He expressed his belief that the decision would be "quite as pernicious" as *Dred Scott,* that it would stimulate aggressions on Negro rights, and worse, would "encourage the belief that it is possible, by means of state enactments, to defeat the beneficent purposes" of the postwar amendments. And he went on to describe the future of segregation in these words:

Sixty millions of whites are in no danger from the presence here of eight millions of blacks. The destinies of the two races, in this country, are indissolubly linked together, and the interests of both require that the common government of all shall not permit the seeds of race hate to be planted under the sanction of law. What can more certainly arouse race hate, what more certainly create and perpetuate a feeling of distrust between these races, than state enactments, which, in fact, proceed on the ground that colored citizens are so inferior and degraded that they cannot be allowed to sit in public coaches occupied by white citizens? That, as all will admit, is the real meaning of such legislation as was enacted in Louisiana.

Justice Harlan clearly saw the path marked by the institutions of the federal system, once the Court upheld the competence of the states "to regulate," as he put it, "the enjoyment by citizens of their civil rights solely upon the basis of race." It is important to remember, however, that the direction taken was not inevitable. Our task is to reverse it, and to make the reversal work, but to do so within the framework of the same institutions.